Wild Things

*There are some who can live without wild things,
and some who cannot.*

—Aldo Leopold

Wild Things

by Dion Henderson

Illustrations by Meryl Meisler

Tamarack Press
P.O. Box 5650
Madison, Wisconsin 53705

Also by DION HENDERSON

A Season of Birds
The Waltons: The Bird Dog
The Wolf of Thunder Mountain
On the Mountain
Hunting
The Last One
Algonquin

Edited by Jill Weber Dean.
Designed by Patricia Dorman.
Jacket designed by Karen Foget.
Jacket photograph by Paul Shane.
Typeset by Guetschow Typesetting.
Printed in the United States of America
    by Wm. C. Brown Company.

First printing 1979.

Library of Congress Cataloging in Publication Data

Henderson, Dion, 1921-
    Wild things.

    1. Zoology—Addresses, essays, lectures.
2.   Natural history—Addresses, essays, lectures.
I.   Title.
QL81.H45   591   78-9687
ISBN 0-915024-18-7

For the snows of yesteryear,
and for Amy and Jane and Bruce and Charles,
who made tracks in them.

Contents

Winter

You cannot shoot a pine knot, or eat it,
but it is a lovely thing and makes a fire
that will burn the bottom out of a stove
if you are not careful. . . . Once I gave an artist
a sack of pine knots and he refused to burn them
and rubbed and polished them into wondrous
birdlike forms, and many called them art. Me,
I just pick them up and burn them.

                              — *Gordon MacQuarrie*

$\mathcal{N}$ow the red leaves as well as the green have gone, and it is time to rest. The days' gradual shortening toward the minimum of the winter solstice has slowed the breath of life itself.

The elms stand tall and brittle; you must put your thumbnail into the smooth bark of a twig to catch a glimpse of green, the promise that the great tide of life will rise again. The toad has dug his own grave and settled into it, jeweled eyes fixed on the sky until the dirt closed over him. In a snug corridor at the end of the long hall that opens on our lawn, the gopher clan is sleeping. It is easier to find a sign of life within the tree than within the other two. For the toad is only an inert lump now, and the gophers are cold, cold, cold. Their hearts move hardly once a minute, stirring their sluggish blood, and they have not enough breath to fog a mirror.

Sometimes, and no one knows how often, among the sleepers, the bright flame burns low and lower and quietly gutters out. Once, a gopher was brought in, curled stiff in that middle state between life and death. When resuscitation seemed fruitless, it was refrigerated and forgotten—until the refrigerator door was opened to sputter and flash and scurry. Life had come back.

This time of resting leaves its mark, however. On some, the mark is sharp and clear. The rings making up a log tell its years. Particularly in ash and oak, less so in maple, you can see the wide light growth of the fat springtime and the darker ring of summer's hardening off. The time of rest shows in absence; there is no growth in winter, and nothing is added to the ring.

The same story is told on the bluegill's scale. As it grows, ridges form around the scale's edge. When metabolism slows, in cold water, the ridges are crowded one atop another. In dead winter, when growth stops, the ridges are incomplete. In spring, growth starts suddenly, cutting across the incomplete ridges. You can count the winter ridges on the scale to age the fish.

In catfish, which have no scales, you can count the years in the rings on a pectoral spine. On other fishes, an ear bone or a vertebra will serve. The ridges on the mussel's shell show its growth by seasons, and annual lines are formed on the shell of some turtles. The age of deer can be determined by examining the cementum layers on the roots of the teeth.

So even rest leaves its mark. Man himself must bear winter's scar, if nowhere else, upon his spirit.

*T*he juncos are back, riding ahead of an onrushing barometric low like youngsters on their sleds. With them, chickadees are frolicking in the spruce around the freshly filled feeders. And cheerfully among these most cheerful of birds is a fat happy lout of a nuthatch. New seeds in the feeder serve as an ancestral welcome, although these birds probably prefer bug or beetle probed from beneath rough bark, and thus will use suet. But they are old friends, under the impression that they have come far enough south to enjoy a mild winter. And so, perhaps, they have, all things being relative.

The nuthatch, whether full size or compact model, is more of a comic than the others, bigger and broader and with a bobtailed construction that makes his long straight bill seem longer still. His tail, or the shortage of it, has a special importance to his operation. If it were long and stiff like a woodpecker's, the nuthatch would look much more like a woodpecker to the casual eye. But his beak is too straight and light for drilling, even if he had the tail for it.

So our nuthatch follows a fleeing bug around a horizontal branch, as comfortable upside down as right-side up. Head down on the bottom of the branch, it sees the nearby observer, makes a polite noise, and whisks on around to another perch. I do not know whether the secret is entirely in the tail assembly, but a nuthatch can run headfirst down a tree as fast as it can run up, something no woodpecker can do. On the other hand, a chickadee does very well in both directions and has a handsome tail as well.

It is useful to know in advance that the sound a nuthatch makes when addressing a person sitting nearby is in the nature of initiating dialog, and many will respond to quiet conversation. But this bird is a songbird only by courtesy and the biological fact of its vocal structure; the sound it emits is something like that made by a little girl who puts her hand into an old winter coat and grasps a live mouse, only not so loud.

No matter, though. The chickadees can sing enough for both, and between them, there is a new busybody brightness to cheer the gray days' advancing. It is only strange to note how readily comes the congeniality between bird and bird, and how hard between man and man.

15

*A*rmed with saw and hatchet, we venture to mingle with the crowd of spruce on the terrace. The blue-green ranks are thick on the slope, the million bristly fingers of their branches interlocked in a dense barrier against blundering invasion. And invasion, let it be known, is why we came; to claim payment for the rental of this slope by a generation of trees and those that dwell within the thicket. It is a large community—mouse and rabbit, chickadee and nuthatch and junco, a hundred kinds of bug and beetle in season—for owl and crow cannot penetrate the formation. Even pussycats must slither along the ground and then be caught and caught again by the brittle triggers of the dead branches lowest on the trunks.

In summer it is cool and moist beneath this shade. And now at Christmas it is warm—warm, at least, by any ready comparison afield. The wind gushes, snow laden, from the northwest, but the spruce only sigh, the candles of the last year bending. Within the thicket the snow loses its velocity and sifts gently down upon the duff. All this, of course, is among the reasons the spruce grow here. They were planted not so long ago on this barren ground to generate a thriving village. They have done so and have further flourished to the point where they can serve a more selfish purpose for their landlord.

They crowd so thickly upon one another now that it is time for some to go, that the others may grow still larger. This, too, was planned, so the needful thinning should coincide with the yuletide. Thus the landlord might do as he did when he was young, a hundred years ago, and cut his own Christmas tree again on his own acreage, not only propitiating his ego but causing the shades of the old tree-worshipping ancestors to draw close to the edge of the firelight in the living room and smile. There is time, while growing spruce trees from seedlings to ten feet high, to conjure on such things.

But master plans often go awry for the very reason of their complexity; they take so long to execute. The children battle with me against the closeness of the spruce grove. A tree of suitable height is singled out, sawed, and hauled free from its clutching companions. But once it is free, the triumph dims. The boys look on the prize with dismay. There is a brown platform of dead branches at the bottom, a great vacancy where a strong brother stifled the growth on this side, a crookedness where ice tipped a leader and another took over, a clear gap in the middle testifying to splendid growth in a wet, warm spring.

My sons are the soul of courtesy, under the circumstances, but the message is plain: I have spent fifteen years courting this dismal prize while one infinitely superior can be purchased from the smirking profiteer on the corner for a little cash and no effort at all. So be it. Sometimes defeat comes easy. The young judge with a deadly eye, and tradition is no substitute these days for quality.

*F*or some weeks, a couple of mice had been wallowing in forbidden pleasures in the backyard, all unseen. A snowbank stretched from one of the rose gardens past a young pear tree to the stone wall. Under the pressures of repeated thaws and sleets, it had condensed and crusted over thickly, roofing the locale of a bacchanalia safe from whatever owl or pussycat might go to see.

But like mice and men before them, this pair grew first fat, then fretful in the soft clutches of security. Aggravated squeakings across the broad range of the meadow mouse's intricate vocabulary were clearly audible to our poodle, whose curiosity waxed exceedingly. He listened for the progress of alarmed *chirruping* and the scrabble of small feet beneath the snow, then plunged through the crust after the fugitives.

Shortly, the snowbank was well plowed, and the roof had fallen in on the world these particular mice had known a substantial part of their lives; for, in nature, the meadow mouse rarely endures more than a year. But a meadow mouse lives a full life in the time allotted him. An infant for a week, he may be a parent in a month—and without interruption thereafter. He will eat his own weight daily if sufficient food is available.

How much mouse damage is ascribed to rabbits, I know not, but it is an easy mistake to make. The mouse works his subversions beneath the shields of grass and darkness in summer, and snow in winter. The rabbit, by contrast, can be caught red-handed when you will. Flip the yard-light switch and there he is, startled ears askew, mouth stuffed with the evidence, and not the grace to look guilty. Thus the beleaguered householder, once he scents attack, may defend with foil and wire against one enemy while another munches under and through his defenses, not the least discommoded.

Unless memory fails, Ruth Hine established that ten meadow mice per acre can consume one hundred pounds of greenery a year. But I do not recall that Dr. Hine established any method of restricting the population to ten. You either have mice or you do not. And if you do, at quadrennial intervals, you have more mice than you expected. There is, in truth, one prompt and effective method to use against an irruption of meadow mice, and that is a Siamese tomcat. This, like other simple solutions to complex problems, has certain disadvantages, as in eliminating a nest of hornets in the attic by burning down the house. For although a Siamese tomcat can cope with anything up to and possibly including an enraged water buffalo, he himself can be coped with by few mammals—poodles, perhaps, and mothers-in-law. And the manner of coping with either of the latter is not known to ecologists at this writing.

19

*I*n new snow, the tracks go blithely across the yard in the lee of the hedges, pausing here to investigate a tuft of grass, there to sniff at a small pile of brush. The tracks are like those of a small dog, but narrower and haired, and showing the marks of sharp claws. There may be fewer rabbits on the premises this winter but they will be more alert, for if we do not have a new resident fox, at least we are booked for occasional appearances.

Although a red fox may travel as much as twenty miles when hunted hard, which is considerably farther than most hunters will push him these days, he's a home-loving soul and normally ranges only a couple of miles from his den. But we have come to the dead of winter, when tender emotions begin to stir in the hearts of foxes and a few other hardy creatures. My transient may be only prospecting and, with four-legged vixens scarce in the neighborhood, may not come this way again.

The red fox, by and large, has been notably successful coexisting with man. Although his numbers have been fairly stable for the last couple of decades, they once swung in great extremes, probably following the cyclic irruptions of rabbits. For foxes depend on rabbits almost as squirrels depend on nuts, and, for Reynard, only an extraordinary fecundity among mice would make up for a dearth of cottontails.

Those who seek simple answers for complicated problems of ecology would make the fox the villain in game-bird and song-bird depletions, as once they blamed him for deviltry in the hen house. Occasionally a fox may develop such perilous tastes, and is likely to pay the penalty; but for foxes in general, mammals make up ninety percent of the menu, with mice making up half the total in season, and rabbits half of it the year round. My fox, for instance, will eat more grapes than pheasants, and more apples than either.

The red fox and the gray are different animals. Old fox-hunters claimed that not only their dogs but they personally could smell the difference at a den. The gray is a poor-pelted tree-climber; the red is sire to all the splendid variations from platinum to silver. He comes, as they say, in every color but white. White pups were born, the old hunters said, but were generally born dead, and biology adds nothing to folklore.

Biology, by the way, has little effect on folklore anyway, when it comes to foxes. This vain little gamin is a successful competitor, and thus, despite his usefulness, his service, and his splendor, men keep dogs to hunt him. And few will understand why, if that track doesn't come across my field again, I will stand diminished.

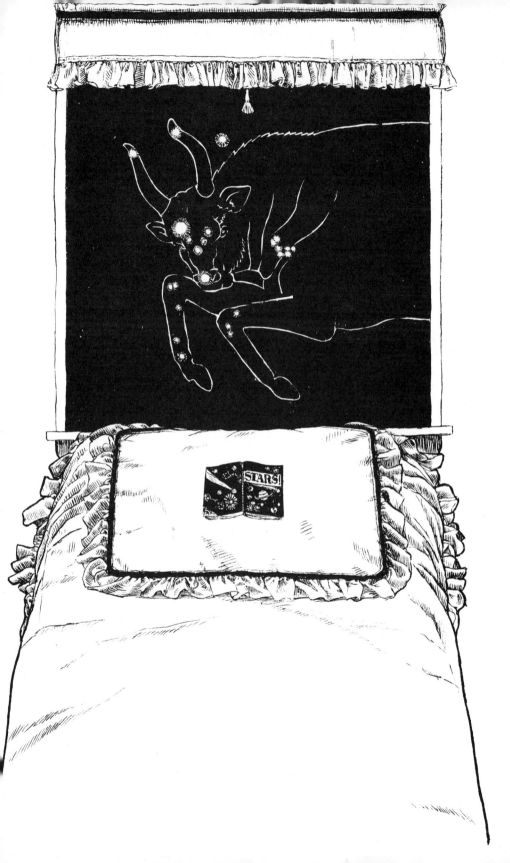

*F*or the young, star watching belongs to summer and sweet-scented grass and the lush constellations of August. When you are no longer quite so young, what is needed is a window to the south. Then you can place your bed just so and, in the long winter night, lie snugly, watching the great pursuit wheeling across that southern sky. A man whose abilities and inclinations lead him rarely to the companionship of astrophysicists may reflect on many things at such a time.

When the intergalactic expeditions master transmission of matter at the speed of light, it will take less than nine years to send a spacecraft swinging among the unknown worlds circling the incandescent hell of Sirius, the nearest sun besides our own. But meanwhile, Sirius is a dog to me, as it was to shepherd boys two thousand years ago.

And there is Taurus, commemorating the bull, whose form the king of the Greek gods borrowed to impress one earthly maiden or another. Below the blazing red eye that is Aldebaran, Taurus wears the Hyades like a V upon his forehead, and the Pleiades like a spangle on his shoulder. For slumbrous contemplation, it is well to remember that the Pleiades once were the seven daughters of Atlas. Counting them is a test of visual acuity yielding more self-satisfaction than any optometric chart devised.

But to look at the Pleiades with even the comparatively low magnification of binoculars is to spoil the illusion and have the myth escape; for, in the glass, the hundred or more stars of the cluster leap startlingly into existence, and the seven lonely sisters are lost in a swarming multitude of lesser lights.

Yet nowhere is it easier for a man who believes only what he sees to be rudely reminded that he sees very little of what is there, and *that* imperfectly and only for a little while. Consider the Egyptian tomb makers, who aligned entrances so that the spirit inside might look out eternally at immortal Thuban, the hub of the universe. But now, only a few thousand years hence, we know Thuban only as a star in Draco, if we know it at all, and guide our ships by Polaris as though it would endure forever. And when the space vehicle that is our earth has wobbled on its way for another ten thousand years, the pole star will be Vega, which blazes overhead in summer.

So much for the majesty of men and the constancy of stars.

*I*n heavy snow, my evergreens stand each according to its character and habit, but all silently and with stoic calm, awaiting a change of wind or return of the sun. By their form and posture you may know them.

The junipers, of course, were overwhelmed by storm. Except for a feathery branch emerging here and there, their line might be a long drift. The thick tough branches that once were considered passable bowwood, except for a tendency to take a set, bow down sullenly beneath the snow. And underneath the branches, there are many-footed revels as the mice disport, safe beneath branch and drift from prowling cat or plunging fox.

But the serried ranks of spruce stand like so many tepees, the sharp four-angled needles on the bristled twigs drooping only imperceptibly under the weight of snow, each branch holding what it may, then letting the surplus slide on down, creating at the heart of each tree a dim shelter for junco, finch, and chickadee.

The cedars would do likewise; they have the heart but not the stomach for it. Their tall spires maintain a stern upright stance until the scaled aromatic leaves have more than they can bear. Then suddenly the whole tower bends under the weight, sometimes almost to the ground, yet only rarely does one break. A hungry deer may thus find an exceptional lunch brought within reach, but brushing against it may dislodge the snow and let the tree snap straight again.

The big trees are different, and different from one another. Shouldering against the storm, the white pines disdain the snow. Their great clusters of long needles, five together and nearly five inches long, wave away accumulation. And when the wind dies, they will remain free, except sometimes for a reticulation of snow driven into the fissures of their curling purple bark.

On the other hand, the Norways grieve at violence. The great branches with their plumes of dark doubled needles sigh at the coming of the wind; and when they are heavy with snow, the branches bend this way and that, unpredictably, creating a haven for huddling beast or even man, away from the cutting edge.

In a way, each of these conifers is the same, yet each behaves according to a pattern that is distinct. Trees, like men, respond to adversity with individuality, and yet predictably, each one according to its nature and the way life has shaped it.

25

*A*t the brush pile in the hedge corner, the dog stops precipitously and, with the splendid transmission given to poodles, shifts smoothly into reverse. She would assail a Bengal tiger in language that the clergy does not know, but her intuition commands her suddenly and with great authority to caution. She backs away fifteen feet. Strangely, that is almost exactly the limit of safe approach—never mind how I know. But what informs this particular dog while failing to inform others?

There is no question about the identity of the handsome fellow in the brush pile. The dog followed the ambling trail in fresh snow, the plantigrade tracks—the big hind feet outside the narrower marks of the front feet, whose claws had dragged—meandering hopefully from rubbish cans to bird feeders and thence to brush pile. No white hunter is needed to explain all this. Let whosoever has a nose use it. The sulfur compound that analysis identifies as n-butylmercaptan provides all the credentials any skunk needs.

The skunk is not a common visitor in winter, but not rare, either, for the tribe follows a plan that might be the envy of any commuter. If the weather is not fit to be abroad, the sensible skunk will sleep it away, venturing out again only when prospects brighten or curiosity beckons. The animal is no true hibernator. And here, with skunks as well as poodles, the feminine mystique has an inexplicable effect: Females are more likely to sleep longer, and more often, than males. Thus, they may be snoozing comfortably away while mankind, on a day of thawing, sniffs the skunky air and says it presages the coming of spring. And so it does, for a reason little known. On mild winter days, when the footcandles of daylight are increasing, boisterous male skunks are abroad, disputing with one another for territory.

A skunk fears practically nothing in nature, but this is a form of brinksmanship that leads more often to disaster than the fearful witness might expect. What will attack a skunk depends not only on ignorance but on hunger. Fox, coyote, bobcat, all will suffer in order to be fed. And great horned owls are not particularly averse to skunk musk; they are the great predators on the clan.

This overconfidence sometimes leads to an even more dismal termination. Skunks are among the leading victims of rabies, largely because they densely stand their ground when some poor mad beastie runs through the woods, sowing the seeds of certain death in flecks of thick saliva. Thus, where fox and cat—and poodle—dodge and flee the unknown, skunks are bitten and infected.

Spring

Now is the moment
when the secret of life could be discovered,
but no one finds it.
— *Donald Culross Peattie*

*T*his is the season, when your feet are wet with it and it puddles in the backyard and creeps into your basement, to think of water. It is the time, when you are standing bleakly in an icy torrent trying to hack open the frozen culvert that is flooding your driveway, to reflect that the cosmic energy utilized in turning one part of this ice back into water would be enough to raise the temperature of a similar amount of water to 176 degrees. Or to consider that of all liquids, this one expands suddenly and unaccountably as it freezes, which is the reason your favorite lake has fish in it instead of forming a solid block of ice. For although water contracts and grows denser and sinks as it cools, at the point of freezing, it expands toward the density of ice. Thus ice floats and is formed only at the top of your lake, never at the bottom.

Water is everything to all who live, and yet we so rarely think of this simple thing that makes us possible—this triangle of two hydrogen atoms and one oxygen atom. Elements that are so flighty alone are, when combined as water, eternal and very nearly immutable. The freezing of water and the boiling of it are incredibly expensive from the standpoint of energy required, yet they are all for nothing because, left alone, water will return to water.

When water is released it spreads, not, for instance, like the self-sufficient globules of mercury but by taking part in whatever it comes in contact with, always participating but never devouring— and never really changing. This is the reason you can dry the floor with a mop or your feet with a towel. It is also the reason the rain that soaks down into the earth does not stay there and leave the world above to wither away in dust. For water will rise of itself, more than twice as high as any other liquid, from grain to grain and from cell to cell, even through tough walls. Fifty feet of maple in my yard says clearly that it does and shows the wet drip of sweet sap for evidence.

This is the time of year for dark miracles, and the rise of water in the trees is one of the darkest. Weeks ago, it must have started. In January, a molecule moved in the frigid night, and the whole cycle started over again. There was upward movement, along the rootlets, then higher—and not only in the maple but in the dogwood growing red and supple and in the greening willow—to the utmost tips.

Later on, the leaves will be transpiring, and their loss of water will pump more sap up to them. But what spoke deep in the earth in January, that the sap should run in March?

31

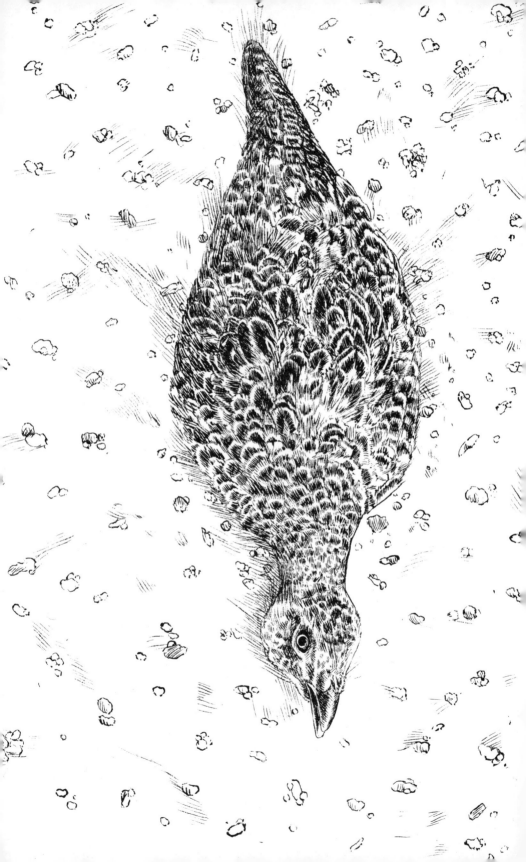

*B*eside the highway, where oil-blackened snow has retreated from the salt-encrusted shoulder of the road, a hen pheasant, victim of a speeding car, lies dead. At home, the sparrows scratch busily in the limestone of the drive, hopping between puddles and patches of dirty ice. It is all for the same reason: In the utter dregs of the year, the mothers of the race begin to think of a new generation, and in the newly exposed gravel of the road shoulders and the limestone of the driveway, they seek the raw material of eggshells and desire to be about their business.

This is one of the eternally sustained promises that spring will come again, but there is a contradiction to it. Among wild things, the vernal equinox comes as the tolling of a funeral bell. In the utmost extremity of privation, when winter's food is gone and summer's bounty still is far away, they must gather their raveled resources and, while death is only a breath away, concentrate on the giving of new life. Yet this is nature's way, and it is relentlessly efficient. Let no sensitive soul attribute mercy to nature; there is none there. The laws of ecology are immune from social amendment.

In the plant world, the making of seed comes at the great, rich, burgeoning end of summer, and the seed is made in countless quantities. With plants, it is the seed that must stand the test of survival—the icy darkness, the cold that lulls the germ asleep, the multitude of hazards that are applied before there is a single sprout from among the thousands.

But among the birds, the rabbits, and the deer, the appointed hour strikes when few are able to answer. Those few, however, have survived the harshest tests of merit. When examples of creatures who have failed are displayed before the eyes of man and he must face the dread reality, he can hardly bear it. In the cedar swamps, for instance, lie the dead deer—those too thin to stand the cold, too weak to avoid the hungry predators, too young or too old or too foolish to balance on their hind feet to reach a browse line six feet above the snow.

But this is how it has to be. Only the best are entitled to produce the new race; all but the best are swept relentlessly away to make room for it.

On one of the first warm days, when the bloodroot's flag is still furled and a lean robin tags hopefully at my heels to spy a beetle or a frosty worm, as I lift mulch from the young perennials, there is a swirl of somber splendor in the sun. It is a butterfly, wearing the richly funereal vestments of the mourning cloak.

A symbol of spring it is, but not an early dividend of life's new season. This nymphalid, dark and comely as Sheba's queen, is a veteran of the winter's wrath as much as the robin and I. And just as glad, no doubt, in her own way, to see the sun god rising higher from his grave each day.

Her clan is one of the largest among the family of true butterflies, and although her relatives have a bewildering variety in color and patterns and in the shapes of their wings, you may know them easily. They are called the four-footed butterflies because their forelegs are too small for walking, resembling small brushes in the males and, if you please, small combs in the females. Among these butterflies are many that sleep the winter away in conventional comfort. The regals may pass the winter as eggs or as first-stage caterpillars; the red admirals may hibernate either as adults or as pupae; and the crescent spots, as larvae.

But then there are the stubborn ones, like my mourning cloak and like the anglewings, which refuse to wither with the waning year. They creep into a crevice, beneath curled bark, inside a hollow limb, and wait. The fire must burn low indeed, and many a stiff, cold creature that feeds a hungry, foraging woodpecker. Yet there are always some nymphalids that weather all the cold and feel the sun and wake to stretch their rusty wings in spring.

It is a vernal tonic to be reminded that not only steel and stone can stand against our relentless clime. Enduring may be done as well by things that are frail and beautiful.

35

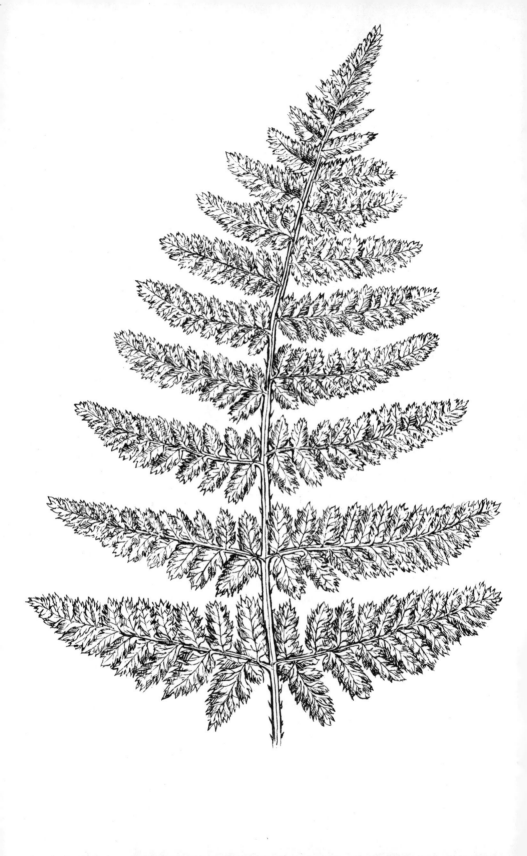

*I*n the cool dampness beside the stone wall, the dead black stumps of the woods ferns explode suddenly in bright new fronds, outcrops of a strange and intricate secret life that is lived in the ageless dark of underground.

From the time when man was very young and ferns already very old, they have been plants of considerable interest—not only for their resurrection of new growth from what appears dead but because of their eerie system of alternation of generations. As in other higher plants, no fern is truly the parent of any other fern; there is a stage between, but the stage appears unrelated.

Our early ancestors, wrinkling a furrowed inch of brow, might have seen in ferns forecasts of great pine forests still to come, not knowing that the ferns had once already ruled the world. Like the birds, ferns had an eon of their own. What now is left is only a fragment of what went before. The age of reptiles was born on a bed of ferns.

But it was in the reproduction of ferns that philosophers thought they saw evidence of spontaneous generation. For an adult fern bears no seeds. Instead, it develops spores, usually along the stalk of a frond. The spores seem like seeds and, also like seeds, germinate if given moisture. But spores do not grow into ferns.

It is hardly a hundred years since plant biologists traced this complicated path of generation. Each spore develops into a small, green, heart-shaped plant called a prothallium, which bears on its lower surfaces the organs of both sexes. But neither does the union of germ cells form seeds; instead, they develop directly into another fern, with enough intricacies to dizzy a geneticist.

And when it is all done, the only part of a fern's life that may be equated with subsequent plants is the leaf alone. All the rest— root, stalk, branch—lie buried in the rootstock. Even today, studying a fern is like staring into the dark depths of a hundred million-year-old past, when huge lizards with tread like thunder walked the earth and what now is coal was lush and green and strange.

37

A plump green fly lands on a stone beside the pool and rubs its forelegs together as though congratulating itself over some deed well done. There is a sound like the snapping of small fingers, and the fly vanishes. Because the disappearance of flies seldom is accomplished by incantation, green leaves around the stone are lifted to determine whether there is a guest in the garden. There is. Beneath a drooping leaf sits a toad.

As we watch, the jeweled eyes close and seem to sink into the creature's skull. It is part of the swallowing procedure, in which the fly, caught by the snap of that long toad tongue, hinged at front instead of behind, is brought into the mouth and forced down the throat by a series of muscle spasms.

This is a rare and welcome visitor to a garden so close to the city; it is only when my boys note that they have never met a toad socially that I realize how rare. The automobile as an environmental control on populations as divergent as deer, rabbits, and the drivers of other automobiles has been studied extensively, but it also is the reason why city children and toads are strangers.

For once, it is not the car itself that kills so many. Instead, it is the modern highway embankment, with its splendid ditches, that takes a tremendous toll of migrating toads. These ditches fill with water in the spring and attract amphibians of all manner of stripe, then turn into death traps when rains wash down the oily residue of the road, smothering the life therein.

We stroke our toad's chin with a bit of grass as a sign of friendliness. He is welcome to stay a year, or twenty years, as some toads have, in agreeable gardens, all the while paying for their residence with insect-reducing services estimated to be worth as much as thirty dollars a year to the horticulturist. But the horizontal pupils in the jeweled eyes are unmoved.

The puppy thrusts a cold wet nose under the leaf to undo our efforts at hospitality. Possessed with instant jealousy, she sniffs with vulgar directness. Then, before a hand can intervene, she picks up the toad in her mouth and is sorry. A toad's parotid glands, behind the eyes, exude a poison that corrodes the membranes of a dog's mouth. There are other glands in the toad's skin as well. In some toads, the exudate is very strong; a large dog can be killed by mouthing a Colorado river toad.

But life is not always a cool spot under a leaf, and fat juicy bugs sailing by within easy tongue's reach, and smugness based on the capability of extracting severe reparations from any overt enemy. No, though the ability to produce the complex proteins of the poison is a great power on the one hand, it leads on the other to the desirability of including toad skins in many a medicinal recipe, from ancient Chinese physic to the brew of Salem's witches, for the material is a substance akin to digitalis, having a substantial effect upon the heart.

The toad is the lesson, not the pupil. Nature rarely gives greatly without also taking away.

A fat friend intercepts me as I take a spade toward the garden. It is the spade that makes this robin's affection flourish. If I carry a rake, his interest flags; with walking stick, I disturb not even the glaze of his lackluster eye. But today I have the spade, and it turns the soil, and so the robin participates with enthusiasm. If there is no worm, he is taken aback. But he is quick to forgive—especially if the next turning of the earth discloses a juicy monster. In the world of robins, the reason that angleworms were put into the ground is self-evident. Yet the robin's view is not true. The worm was here long before robins or boys with fish poles, and quite likely will endure long afterward.

All of us who depend for sustenance on the fertile soil must acknowledge our basic debt to the worm. His alimentary canal is the path that leads us to food. Our rich dirt is worm-processed a countless million times.

This simple creature built the field that fed Tamerlane and buried his cities. Darwin found that in poor soil, the worm must eat more, and thus work harder at increasing tillable land, than in good soil. Watson reports that in the years since the Romans built their pavement in Britain, the stones have been covered from one foot to two feet deep with dirt, and every grain passed through the bodies of the worms.

Somehow, it is unsettling that so basic and straightforward an animal should be possessed of qualities we cannot satisfactorily explain. One can demonstrate how the tiny bristles on each segment propel a worm through the slime-greased tube of its burrow. We know that worms are eyeless, yet the merest touch of a flashlight's beam falling on a night crawler stretched out long, tail anchoring it to its hole, will touch off a lightning reflex. Snap! The worm vanishes. Blind but not sightless? Or is there a sense we do not know?

It is easier to understand why humanity remains in debt to these tillers and creators of the soil. So far at least, the angleworm has been able to fabricate the stuff of earth faster than wind, water, and man can wear it away.

41

In the small hours of the morning, there is a soundless stirring beside my desk. When the lamp is tipped, there are pale green arrowheads of leaves reaching blindly up the legs of my typewriter table toward the light. The wild morning-glory has come again, with its unbearable tenacity, making plain the case that it was here first and here it will remain, despite all adversaries. From the almost invisible space between the immense stone of the house itself and the slab of concrete that was poured more than a decade ago to make the floor of my den, the incredible statement of faith in the process of life has emerged. I know not how long the bindweed grew here, in this place, before the house came, and after that the concrete, but for a decade it has risen at exactly the same point—fifteen feet from light, from air, from water; sealed off from all the things that fan the sparks of life within the earth; driven, perhaps, as Ahab never was, by irresistible forces pressing stubbornly, cell by cell, upward along a vast and uncharted root system.

These roots of the bindweeds bear examination. They are white and hard, and resist the earthworm-style fragmentation that has given quack grass its unenvied record of pernicious multiplication in the face of adversity. But once I took away a bank where bindweeds flourished in an old garden, and five feet down in the red clay, the one root of each had become a dozen, and still they went down. And when the red clay was purified by arsenites, and stone was put upon it for a terrace, promptly the bindweeds rose, proliferating from each of the subterranean rootlets, to make you think of Medusa's hair.

From the house and lineage that gives us not only the true morning-glory but the sweet potato as well come the bindweeds. There are two—my dauntless acquaintance and its hedge cousin, which is called Rutland beauty, thereby suggesting that some of the people who named wild flowers were persuaded more by sentiment than sense. Botanically, bindweeds differ from morning-glories, having two stigmas, among other things, but their character is such that even botanically they are among the disturbance-community specimens that Dr. Curtis would rather not dwell upon when discussing the vegetation of civilized places.

And yet my bindweed comes, again and again, year after year, beyond all expectation, almost beyond all possibility. You could eradicate it, perhaps, as Carthage was destroyed—its males killed, its women and children sold into slavery, its structures burned, its land plowed and sowed to salt. But even then . . .

43

*I*n the arbor, the young grapevines, pruned once to strong single canes, now stand as stubs. The canes lie beside them, snipped cleanly off by sharp white teeth. Rabbit tracks in the wet soil show the purposeful progress of a miscreant from vine to vine—here a pause to adjust the incisors, there a stretch on tiptoe, now a thoughtful pause before moving on to more destruction.

Rabbits do not eat grapevines or their bark, and this rabbit did not have to taste six vines to know he did not like them. In truth, he was not hungry, for there was tender lilac not a yard away; and young peach trees, whose bark is food of choice to nearly all rodents, were available at the other side of the garden. I am reminded of a Norway-pine plantation, a line of four-year-old transplants a quarter of a mile long. One night, for a reason perhaps hidden in the mystery of lunar phases, a neighborhood gang of delinquent rabbits divided up the furlongs and snipped the budding candle from each little pine. Rabbits do not like Norway pine, either, especially when there is white cedar in a row beside it.

This deplorable conduct by the rabbits in my garden is what would pass for vandalism among the juvenile authorities—destruction, just for the hell of it. And although some may be offended by the notion, there is small ground for contradiction. All animals play, like children; why should they not on occasion be naughty or malicious, like children?

There is a bear in fond memory who, when hungry, would rip up a rotten stump to explore for beetles, and, when not hungry, would rip up any handy stump anyway—for practice, for fun, or for some other reason. And a splendid tiger of a pointer dog whose heart overflowed with wrath when he was kenneled. He would not rest until he had torn a hole in the wire and gotten outside, whereupon he would turn around and tear another hole in the wire to get back in. Was it the principle of the thing or something else?

The little brothers on the outside do enough damage, certainly, while about their lawful pursuits—the mouse filling his belly with pear bark while girdling a tree, the birds stuffing themselves with catkins, even the caterpillars munching their way from leaf to leaf. Animal vandalism is another matter, and not so easily dismissed. It may be, after all, that man's talent for deviltry is not so exclusive as our sociologists would have us think.

45

*M*y grandmother used to say that there wasn't room for two females in one kitchen. The same might be said of one garage, particularly if one female is a poodle and one is a raccoon. The spitting and whistling from the rafters there, and the barking underneath, give evidence of a dialogue deteriorating into language employed exclusively by the laity, and a rude segment at that.

This is the risk in leaving a suburban garage door open in the spring, when young raccoons set out to find new homes and set up housekeeping. There is no real migration, for although they may travel thirty or forty miles before settling down, most individuals will range only a couple of miles from the new base thereafter.

Like rabbits, there may be as many raccoons now as there were a hundred years ago, and it must be confessed that to the indignant householder who sallies forth to behold a disaster area where his unguarded garbage cans had stood the night before, there may seem to be too many. It is said, sometimes by people who should know better, that the coon has come to terms with man. In reality, the coon has accomplished a triumph of the sort dear to guerillas. He has continued to dwell, with skill and patience, in his own wild world— which shares the time and place of man's—taking what he pleases and giving nothing back. Not even, it might be noted, one of the really superior furs, for in most quarters raccoon is considered unfashionable.

This, it might be noted parenthetically, has put the ancient American pastime of coon hunting into the amateur class, which may not be an unmitigated loss anyway.

The raccoon can, like the turkey, lay claim to the territory on the grounds that it was here first. Captain John Smith made first formal reference to the coon, reporting a creature that is "like a badger, but vseth to live on trees as squirrels doe," which suggests that the good captain's powers of persuasion exceeded considerably his powers of description. Yet he called it *aroughcun,* possibly a Roanoke word, but one that clearly evolved into *raccoon.* The French voyageurs called the animal *le chat sauvage,* which bespeaks an initial experience that involved a raccoon in a corner, when its normal inclination to ignore man entirely undergoes a ferocious transformation. The coon's family name is Procyon, which also is the name of the Dog Star. And, to be sure, biologically the raccoon is most closely allied with the family of bears, give or take a couple of molars. So there are three choices : cat, dog, and bear. We see what we want to see in the unfamiliar.

The raccoon, of course, cares not a whit. He substitutes tomatoes and watermelon and sweet corn from the garden patch for the acorns and hickory nuts and wild berries of the forest. And he unexcitedly transfers housing, from fifty feet high in a hollow oak to the ceiling of my garage, living in a separate dimension that becomes reality to us only when it impinges on our own.

47

Summer

After much wandering and seeing things,
four snakes gliding up and down a hollow
for no purpose that I could see—not to eat,
not for love, but only gliding.
                    — Ralph Waldo Emerson

*L*ast night the mower left the lawn as green and level as the blotter on my desk, an unmarred sweep of grass victorious. This morning the enemy that ducked its head beneath the whirling blades has sent up a thousand flagpoles from which to flaunt the yellow banners of rebellion. The dandelions have grown stems five inches long overnight—and bloomed. By tomorrow they will have gone to seed, and the seed children will have taken wing on the wind to start new colonies upon, I hope, my neighbor's yard instead of mine.

An old philosopher of my acquaintance long ago would take to brooding that perhaps the Irish daisies would not bloom again. This ominous presentiment came upon him at the time that the barrel in his basement gurgled emptily when one turned the spigot; he had what apparently is a now-vanished medicinal interest in the plant. His magical concoction was variously described as spring tonic, cold medicine, and anti-sea-serpent potion. It may have failed occasionally in the first or second category but to my knowledge was unfailingly successful in the last.

The philosopher need not have worried. This fugitive from the flower gardens of Europe can withstand the worst attacks mounted against it. In our lifetime we may yet find one of its mutant offspring thriving on herbicides. And, of course, it sneers openly at mechanical offensives. The plant itself nestles down there in the grass, where the moisture and the carbon dioxide to build its sugars are most abundant, and stuffs its fat root with still more energy. This root is the reason why decapitation of the plant by an indignant householder is ineffective and why a dandelion can send a budded stipe up above the grass in a few hours.

Dandelion has been used as medicine and, at least to some extent, still is. The thirsty philosopher of my youth had the right idea but the wrong end of the plant. The root is what the old-time druggist cherished. Not so long ago one hundred thousand pounds of dandelion roots were imported each year to be used in the production of tonics and liver medicine. (The philosopher's product was likely to render an ailing liver still more ailing.) And if you can find a patch of dandelions that have not been doused with herbicides or otherwise abused, the tender spring leaves still make better greens than some you find at the produce counter.

At any rate there are ample grounds to speculate that we keep too silent while the grass fancier rants and raves. Any flower whose stew proves out to ten percent alcohol in twelve days cannot be all bad.

A cowbird in modest brown raiment pauses demurely at the pool. A male cowbird veers in, and there is a maidenly flutter. Though a man must be careful of what he says, especially about such things as cowbirds, I am constrained to point out that thoughts of true love must be put aside. While a cowbird consorts only with her friends, she appears not to have an enemy in her whole species.

There is hardly another wild creature so wholly and understandably promiscuous. Yet there are few, wild or otherwise, whose deplorable morals are so well received. Every smaller bird in the yard, and particularly those of virtuous and responsible housekeeping habits, is the potential operator of a foundling home for an orphan cowbird. The foster parents not only will hatch the egg carelessly left among their own but will feed and cherish the intruder while their own young ones starve. They may be seen any time now on the lawn at evening, the harassed host and hostess, followed by a lout of a young cowbird squawking and clamoring to be fed. And each such cowbird represents a brood of lost sparrows or other birds.

The cowbird makes no pretense of building a nest or caring for—or even hatching—her eggs. When nature summons her to deliver the product of her trifling, she leaves her egg wherever she can find room, and she may do it a dozen times a year. Occasionally a small bird will become indignant over the large, strange egg and abandon the whole nest. Even more rarely, it will build a floor atop the first clutch of eggs and start laying all over again. But it may be a losing fight, for the cowbird likely will return. There are records of a warbler nest with three floors and three sets of eggs, each including an unwanted guest.

The cowbird egg hatches sooner than those of perching birds, and the nestling either ousts the eggs that belong there or punctures them or crowds the younger birds out, thus getting all the attention for itself.

The male cowbird is plain enough, dull black and brown-headed, but the ladies in his life are easily mistaken for their respectable blackbird cousins. Named by farmers for their attention to the lowing herds, cowbirds are responsible for many good works that are overlooked. They are very big on grasshoppers and cutworms, they devour weed seeds, and they eschew virtually all cultivated fruits. But in a family that includes the splendor of meadowlarks and bobolinks and orioles, cowbirds form the basis of a perverse maxim. In this case, fine feathers really do make fine birds.

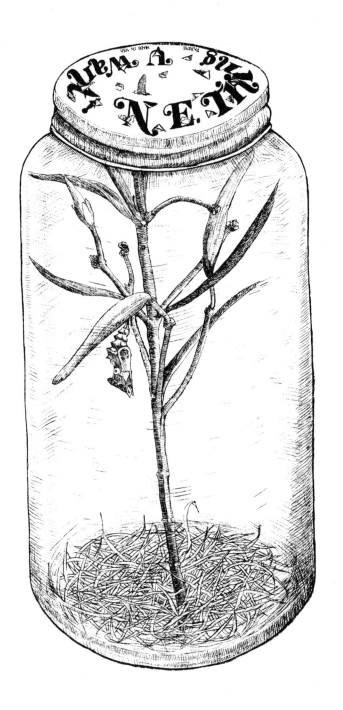

*M*y youngest found a spiny worm the other day and cherished it and brought it home. Safe upon its leaf, it was put in a jar and presently it slept. It was a lackadaisical and poorly ordered caterpillar, going to sleep in a leaf drawn carelessly around it with a strand of silk here, another around the middle, and a little bit about the firm hook from which it dangled by its tail.

By this we knew it was due to be a butterfly, and with only a short wait, instead of one of the huge moths, which putter and fret and deliberate, spin one way and then another, and then fussily do it all over again. There are other differences, too, between these two great occupants of the order Lepidoptera. The butterflies set sail by day; the moths display their glorious raiment chiefly to the moon. Butterfly antennae end in knobs, like the knobs that hang at the end of wires; moths draw their sensations of touch with what look like tiny, graceful feathers.

But this was to be a butterfly, and soon it was—a splendid maroon-and-orange nymphalid called the anglewing for a reason obvious once it perched upon the jar's edge, preparing to launch out upon the air. Instead of smoothly rounded wing lobes, there were serrated edges, as though the wings had been cut from a sheet of color-splashed paper by a capricious child.

My youngest watched, dazzled, as his stepchild gained the air. Then he took apart the untidy cocoon and examined the frowsy caterpillar suit that had been briefly worn. "I don't blame him," the boy said of the butterfly. "I would be in a hurry, too, if this is what I'd been, and that is what I was going to be."

Our nymphalid, like all its tribe—one of the world's most widely distributed families—shortly after leaving its pupal case had ejected a sizeable drop of red fluid. It still marked the jar, like a drop of blood. This is the butterfly that, in ancient times in its massed flight, was the source of the "red rain," the "blood falling from the sky," that struck with fear the superstitious souls of primitive people, or stirred in them the zealots' fever, according to their consciences and their culture, and caused them to cower or set up temples or slay their fellow man, thus binding themselves and their children more closely to engulfing ignorance.

Sometimes knowing is such a little thing. A pharaoh might have changed the course of history if only he had once been a seven-year-old boy with a spiny worm to watch.

*T*he boys have a new sensation: Reporting together and individually, attesting to one another's veracity, they have compiled a biological record indicating that in the bank behind the gardens, residence has been established by either a small grizzly bear or a large woodchuck. The eyewitness accounts, especially from the six-year-old, tend to favor the possibility of the bear, but the hole—gaping and mysterious enough, but something you can measure and see that it is wider than it is high—favors the woodchuck.

There is an implication here having to do with the value of eyewitness reports, and it is not limited to little boys, as any accident investigator as well as any biologist can tell you. You do not see very much, really, unless you know what you're looking for.

And so we look, at the dust outside the hole, and at the edge of the garden, and find one of the startling prints that looks like the hand of a small simian child, for the marmot has a vestigial thumb. And if we look toward garden or clover patch at early morning or at twilight, we may see our fellow landholder himself, either reddish or gray, with a short bushy tail and a midsummer waddle that tells you why his hole is shaped the way it is.

Though scarcely a fantastic creature, the woodchuck is a prime example of the fantasy through which humans so often people their outdoor world. Because of the nonsense of Groundhog Day's effect on the weather, the woodchuck is talked about enough to be familiar to everyone, and yet is not familiar at all.

Perhaps it was always so, for, from the time the settlers came, the chuck made an ally out of man, but never a friend. A creature naturally of the forest edge, he readily shifted from a hole dug between the protecting roots of a tree to a hole under the granary floor and now to a den burrowed into a rock terrace beside our garden. A home-loving soul, he lives his life within a radius of two hundred or three hundred feet. And except in the spring, when hunger keeps him stuffing away fresh and succulent greenery, you must rise early and keep a sharp watch to see him about his business or hear more than a sharp whistle.

Eating is a serious business in spring, for he is one of the true sleepers and may hibernate five months or more. The fire burns very low in that time. A woodchuck's temperature may sink to within five degrees of freezing, and he may lose forty percent of his weight just keeping the ice from forming in his veins. On about Groundhog Day, nature's alarm bell may ring and wake the woodchuck from his deathly trance. Unlike some others, who would starve if wakened before their food supply were ready, the chuck aroused in February can take a look at all the icy white, go back to his bedroom, turn down the thermostat, and sleep again. (And if it is February, whether the sun shines or not, we will have six more weeks of winter. At the very least.)

But now, in summer, that is all behind the woodchuck, or all ahead, and he wallows in the largesse of the in-between.

*T*here is a flicker of orange and black near the tall, succulent stalks of milkweed. A hungry blue jay swoops perilously near the viceroy butterfly but misses—on purpose I think. From time immemorial, jays have abjured the real monarch butterfly because its larvae characteristically feed on a milkweed whose thick juices are toxic and unpalatable. Yet a team of scientists once found that monarch larvae, those smooth chartreuse caterpillars with the filaments on each end, could be taught to eat cabbage rather than milkweed, and that young blue jays then could be taught to eat the larvae. This discovery had in it the seeds of scientific sensation, except that it became known that blue jays need not be taught; they will volunteer happily to dine on monarch caterpillars that have in nature been gorging on milkweed other than the poisonous variety.

All this was an interesting by-product of the real goal of the experiment, which was aimed at solemn medical questions about how far away in the food chain from the terminus where they are identified and blamed pathogens actually originate. (Is it possible, for instance, that cholesterol originates not in the egg but in the chicken feed? Or before that?)

But we stray from the life and time of butterflies and blue jays. One of the latter sits on an apple branch, beady eye on the orange-and-black wings that had been only coincidentally near the milkweed, for the viceroy, or false monarch, has no particular interests there. The jay's concern, though, raises another question. The viceroy lives generally free of danger from birds, some people think, because of its resemblance to the toxic monarch. And some have taught that this is an example of mimicry in nature, whereby a nymphalid that really is a tasty morsel has come, through evolution, to resemble a butterfly that most birds know is not.

The notion is mentioned here but not supported, for while reflection proceeded, the viceroy in question wandered away from the milkweed into the garden, and the watching blue jay swooped again—and did not miss. Thus it is with theories.

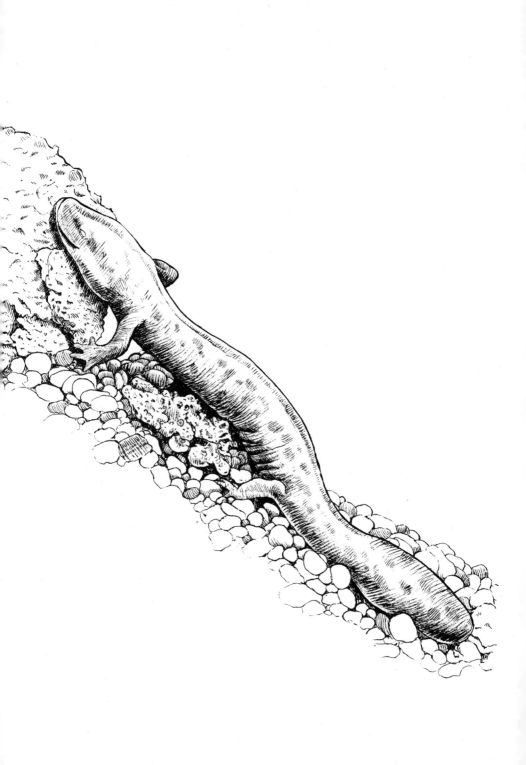

*F*rom the yowl of mortal anguish coming from the dark weedy shoreline, we were about to lose the youngest fisherman in the family. And so we were, although not to some monster of the deep; though, on the other hand, that might have been a fair description. At any rate, a rescue party set out and presently located our youngest, sheet white in lantern light, pointing in wordless horror at his catch—a common mud-puppy. Even a hint of amusement would have been a grave error in judgment, marital as well as paternal. The fisherman's mother was, instantly and wholeheartedly, on his side and, with her superior training and experience, can yell even louder.

In truth, fainthearted or not, this little salamander is nothing to encounter for the first time on a warm summer night. It is always with us, yet little known. As a matter of fact, knowing that it dwells familiarly along the beach is enough to make landlubbers of half the family.

Each of the Salamander genera seems to have some characteristic that is bizarre to those who limit their acquaintance to the higher forms. There are lungless salamanders, which must breathe through the skin and the membranes of the mouth and which, in addition, have a solid lower jaw. There are those with poisonous skin exudate and those whose legs are vestigial or less. Then there is our mottled friend, the water dog—so called by our fathers because they were sure he barked although he doesn't.

Among their genuine claims to individuality, the mud puppy and his kinsmen in our hemisphere are perennially larval; they never lose their gills. And they breed without ever really attaining the mature stage, a condition considered far more remarkable before social anthropologists discovered the condition was not only common but chronic in certain primates. Late summer is mud puppy mating time, although the eggs will not be laid and attached singly to the underside of pier posts or underwater rocks until the following spring.

The mud puppy, with very little to recommend him otherwise, bears a message for the field naturalist in strange waters. In cold, fresh water his gills are tight and contracted; as the water warms, and especially as its oxygen content is lowered by pollution, his gills expand until they make an eerie dark-red ruff of plumes around his neck. Yet on this night, the lesson is lost. Sometimes it is too much even to *face* reality, to say nothing of learning from it.

*A*n impasse has been attained between me and the bumblebee that dwells beside the barbecue. She has deprived me of full title to the lower terrace, but someday she will waddle a bit too slowly into the tunnel between the bricks. Whack, the place will belong to me again. And it had best be soon, before her golden daughters begin to swarm.

A bumblebee has no business setting up a household in a brick apartment beside the barbecue. Having made her marriage flight in autumn and endured winter in a crevice or burrow, in springtime the bumblebee usually finds a field mouse hole and moves in. The field mouse of mature judgment thereupon moves the hell out. The bumblebee then builds a nest of pollen, deposits the eggs fertilized half a year ago, and builds a honeypot for storage.

All this is in early spring. A bumblebee may lurk in the burrow for days on end when the weather turns chill or fretful, perhaps incubating, but she is at work as soon as possible. This dreadnaught of the bee tribe is primarily a pollen collector. When she forces the portals of a flower, it is for the dusty stuff of life, primarily, and any service done the flower is done inadvertently, as is usual in nature's schemes.

Meanwhile, back at the burrow, the eggs hatch into larvae. The larvae gorge on pollen, which, as a special treat, the old bee occasionally mixes with a moistening of honey, then drape themselves in the winding sheet of a cocoon to prepare for wings. They will be up and about by midsummer, and mature by fall, but only fertilized females will survive the winter.

Thus it is with the best-laid records of behavior, but my bee is still secure behind the bricks at the barbecue, and if she does not thrive on smoke and the fumes of malathion, at least she has not been discouraged. The pioneer who would move from a familiar environment to a strange one, as a bee moving from burrow to bricks, must be ready for trouble. Few creatures are more ready than a bumblebee.

I remember the long-ago teacher who, holding a bumblebee between thumb and forefinger to point out thorax and segmentation, was murderously stung. Asked if his assailant had been a *Bombus horribilis,* he snarled, "Yes." So in my mind this has continued to be the grizzly bear of bees. If she will stick to her bricks, she may have them. There are times when a man is happy to settle for an impasse.

*T*he householder who, foraging in early morning with cereal bowl in hand, finds a late strawberry here, a cherry there, and presently a flourish of black raspberries may be inclined to reflect upon the largesse of the land. But it is well to temper the gratitude for a fruitful nature with the recollections that the strawberry is made possible by stringent quarantines, the raspberry is the product of countless generations of selectivity, and the cherry is here at all only because a plant biologist found a stock that could be grafted compatibly between the bearing fruitwood and the rootstock, which makes it possible to grow in our climate but upon which the cherry will not grow directly.

Thus it is with many simple pleasures. Upon more examination they are found to be less simple, but he who would object to such inquiry assumes the position that pleasure must necessarily be diminished by understanding. In fact, comprehension adds another dimension to pleasure, and the thesis is not limited to nature. The son who knows the built-in handicap of the Unicorn hitch and the history of the Lion and Mirror bandwagon has a deeper admiration for the circus parade than the son who still has eyes only for the camels. The musician hears more in great music than I. And there is no way to understand the bittersweet joy of finding a showing of arbutus along the Flambeau without knowing that it takes a hemlock duff one hundred years abuilding to germinate this seed naturally.

But in his search for knowing, it is, perhaps, in nature that a man comes most quickly and insurmountably to the unknowable. This is the direct passage to humility. In ecology, on every hand, at every turn, there is suddenly the darkness of what cannot be explained: the coming of the alewives, the passing of the pigeons, the routine travels of the gray geese, who answer signals we cannot hear and follow signs we cannot read.

If there is a case for the pleasures of determined ignorance, it will have to be put forward by another. But it is harder to make an assessment of the value of knowing and of the value of confronting the unknown. Perhaps the two are only parts of something that man alone in his wild community possesses: the resolution to interrogate and the vanity to consider it important.

*T*he desert candles are blooming now, glowing whitely in the furry darkness of the summer night. Some will last thus three weeks or more; on others, the first-opening flowers are there but for a day. They are handsome enough by day, with the rare color of rich cream, but at night, and especially on dark nights when the sky is pricked only with starlight, they glow luminously the length of the garden. They were so when Remington painted them in his pictures of the Southwest, and the horticultural varieties with us now seem even more richly beaconed amid our comparative lushness.

And if their fairy godmother touches them with her wand tonight, or another night, the stalks will stand sturdily on through frost, and even snow, their hard pods opening only in winter to spread rich black seeds, like small sunflower seeds, enjoyed by cardinals and jays. But the wand must be waved; make no mistake about it. If the fairy godmother of yuccas does not work her magic in the night, there will be no seed.

Tegeticula yuccasella is her name, if you would know the ringing syllable with which to work a spell. She is a small white godmother, primitive as moths go, but beyond price to yuccas. She has mouth parts evolved for this one great work. With them she rolls pollen from the stamens of a yucca flower into a ball, then goes to a new flower. There she deposits an egg deep into the flower, then packs the ball of pollen atop the depression in the pistil. Now the flower will produce seeds. A few of them will be eaten by the moth larva, it is true, but enough will be left so there will be a grateful flash of red or blue against the snow when ripeness comes and the pods open.

Among the three score or so moths, dozens have evolved some odd characteristic of mouth parts, suiting them better to drinking the nectar of one flower order than another. And the flower, in its turn, has developed so that no other moth can do so well at taking the two separate units of the stuff of life and bringing them together to strike the mortal spark. Witness the sphinx moth at the columbine, or the little blue carpenter bee humming angrily as it searches for the way out of the lady's slipper's bloom.

This is the relationship called symbiosis, the dependence of one life form upon another. It can be carried to intricate and even impossible extremes. Perhaps only man feels himself free of such vital links with his environment, feels that he needs nothing beyond that which he himself can create. The mammoth might have something to contribute to such thoughts of racial independence, but the mammoth is very quiet, in the ice.

*F*rom birch to birch to lily pad and pool and back to birch again, an indignant pinwheel gives off blue-and-yellow sparks. The indigo buntings and the goldfinches are concluding a family reunion on the usual terms. From the shining iridescence of the buntings and the smart yellow-and-black habits of the goldfinches, we know that only the males are involved here. Occasionally a canary female in her olive dress takes up a station on the rock above the pool and watches, her head moving like a spectator at a Ping-Pong match as the males whiz by, but no bunting female is visible, unless she is among the sparrows scratching in the dust.

There is some cause to speculate over this fracas of the finches, though the damage is no greater than at most poolside brawls, which is to say, the largest trick involves falling in. At this time of year these two birds are best known for doing things that should keep them out of contact with one another.

The goldfinches should be about their belated business as parents. They are the last of all our songbirds to nest, hardly ever getting to it until June has come, occasionally moving into an old blackbird nest, and then dallying with nestlings well into September.

The indigo birds, on the other hand, should be following no career now but that of entertainers. In late summer, when all the territorial calls are stilled and even blue jays hasten silently past with the look of harried husbands, the indigo buntings are called upon to sing. They are at their best when the mimic thrushes all are silent and the robins stagger in the shade with beaks agape, like television actors in a desert scene.

Yet buntings and goldfinches have much in common, despite the disparity in color. Both are virtually faultless as songbirds, both are dedicated to weed seeds and pernicious bugs, both are companionable to the extreme and ornamental almost beyond belief.

The dispute beside the pool, whatever it was about, is over now. The goldfinches are bathing on the lily pads; the buntings are singing their way up in the birches, beginning their songs on a low branch, then moving up higher for each chorus until they reach the spindly top. A solemn thought occurs: How much better, music lover, to hear these finches sing wild than to hear their trained canary cousins in a cage.

69

Autumn

My September song is still based mainly on the fact that all the tourists went home and left the beaches and the marshes to the Old Man, the eagle, and me.
— *Robert Ruark*

*A*ll at once, or so it seems, the birches by the pool behind the house have turned, the ermine trunks reaching up now into a spray of gold. As though it were a signal, up and down the hills, summer's decent greens have vanished, and the trees burn bright candles to the harvest moon. My younger son says happily, "Jack Frost was here."

He is told that the color in the woods is no bright raiment brought out to celebrate the season, touched up in flaring colors by an elf. It is instead the signal of an autumn fact: Another growing season is done. The beauty means the leaves are dead. Having served their purpose, they died, if you must know, some days or even weeks ago. Already the guarded buds of next spring's popping growth are there along the twigs.

The incredible, individual factories of the leaves have done their work. Their stomata breathed gulps of air and water in and out. In the particles called chloroplasts, the immensely intricate enzyme chemistry of photosynthesis took place, utilizing carbon dioxide and water to form sugars, among them dextrose, from which ninety-five percent of the body of the tree ultimately is made. And only one percent of the solar energy falling on the leaf was utilized for fuel.

There is an efficiency here that has escaped the nuclear people, perhaps because it is hard for them to think of wonders that are no higher above the ground than a treetop. But this leaf, this splendid machine, creates chlorophyll, so similar in structure to the hemoglobin of the blood. Chlorophyll is green, but in reflected light it glows as red as blood. The leaf's dextrines combine with nitrogen to form amino acids, the building blocks of protein, from which all life is made.

In less than five months, the leaf has done what it should do. Then the shortening periods of sunlight signal the end, and the metabolism slows and stops. Then the rare and wondrous vials tip and spill aimlessly. The chemicals run together in the drying leaf—the rare sugars and the catalyzing agents like the enzymes—and the maples put on lemon or vermilion, according to their tastes, and the red flag of the proletariat rises among the sumacs.

"So now," the older boy says to his brother, "you know why the leaves turn?"

"Yes," the younger boy says happily. "Because Jack Frost was here."

I do not find it hard to know why Druids worshipped trees.

*D*ripping wet and gray, dawn comes cool and late in autumn; late enough for even the most tireless reveler to be safely home abed, and depressing enough to make him wish he were, if he is not. But neither the hour nor the rain is dependable when applied to the fleshy weakness of a neighbor, be he man or mouse.

Mine, most recently, was an errant mouse. The dog and I were sitting on the stones, waiting for the sun, when the sporting gallant of the house of rodents and the tribe of *Peromyscus,* which is to say a white-footed mouse, came staggering along the wall. Whether he had celebrated October or the waning of the moon was not clear, but celebrate he had. Hoisting the orange wild plums, bursting sweet with rich sugar and fermenting yeastily now in the wake of frost, he had stood too long at the bar.

The arid voice of temperance falls on deaf ears, even in the wild, at the time of bounty and what Wolfe called the mellow dropping harvest. A man needs no laboratory culture, no esoteric recipes, no incantations, to coax fermentation into life in old October. In that month it comes, the tiny bubbles rising in the juice of life, without such arts or sciences, even in spite of them.

Grape and plum and even apple bear spores of winey turbulence within their skins or close about them; left alone, they form a cider. It does not match the cask's schedule of twelve percent in twelve days, and it bears a foxy taste to turn the purist's nose, but it is all the same to the conventioneering robin, the roistering jay, and yes, to the mouse staggering home by daylight to my wall.

The mouse steps inexactly on the rough edges of the stones. He falls from one and lies a moment on his back, front feet folded on his white vest. If this variety of mouse did more than whistle or make scratchy communicative patter with his front feet, then surely he would giggle.

He rises in drunken joy and chases his tail briefly. He ventures into a chipmunk hole and backs hastily out, unoffended at the inaudible observation made deep within by the householder. He attempts the wall again, tail elevated at the challenge. He is heedless of the danger of full daylight, unaware that nature gives to mice only one moment of foolishness, and sometimes not even that. He does not see the cat crouched waiting for him at the top of the wall.

The cat cares only for the approaching mouse. The mouse cares for nothing. The dog beside me cares only for the cat, and, in turn, I care only for philosophy and seeing how things come out. And if there is a moral in it, here is how it went. The mouse fell off the wall again, the cat moved tensely, and the dog whooped in rage and charged. The cat went up a tree, the mouse went into the wall. It occurred to me that my grandmother, who referred often to the noting of each sparrow's fall, would have been pleased to observe that ratios are still worked out among poodles and pussycats to demonstrate a vested interest even in inebriated mice.

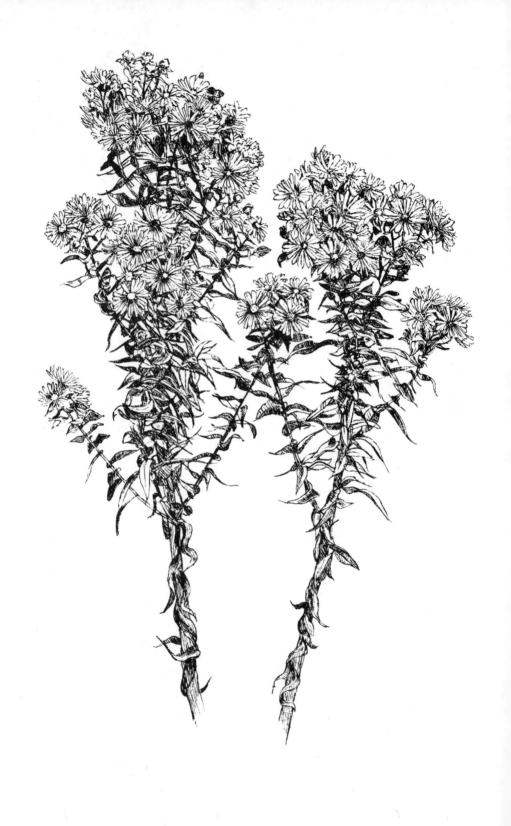

*W*eeds, a friend says, are only flowers growing where you did not plant them. Along the hedges, in the fencerow, and even in the garden corners where cultivation flagged with the waning season, the New England aster showers blue sparks in affirmation. This wild flower—or weed, if you wish—is my favorite among a tribe that must number two hundred species, though the common garden annual is not among them.

Aster means "star" in Latin, hence some classicists still call the family starwort, and the plant is a relative of goldenrod and fleabane. But you do not need to know these things to admire the proud barbarians blooming in the hedge. In its natural habits, the aster is too bold and brash for gardens. Its leaves are rough in your fingers, and it grows five feet high in good ground. It is a hairy, sticky, rude fellow, elbowing even ragweed aside to gain the light, but its flowers are a disciplined praise of autumn. These flowers may range in hue from white to pink to darkest violet. Mine are vivid blue, an inch and a half across, with good gold centers among the delicate frieze of ray flowers.

Like all composites, asters make fruit, thus adding to the larder that the hedge produces. This is of interest to foraging mice and small birds, for whom the tall dry stalks will offer a harvest even in deep snow, but it does not concern me personally; it has nothing to do with the feeling of welcome recognition that comes with the opening of the first bright clusters.

I do not know why it should be so, but if the New England aster must go in order that I should have a clean garden, then I will not have a clean garden. If I must endure burdock and ragweed to keep the aster, then I will sneeze in payment. And I will regard the spraddled holdout in the hedge as a stubborn sermon against the deathly sanitation of wide-spectrum herbicides. There are some problems in the green world, as in others, where solution, however ready, comes at too high a price.

77

*M*y youngest brings me a fine red apple, fallen a day or two ago in the tall wet grass and now the property of a common slug, which clings industriously and obliviously to the great prize and rasps happily away at it while they are both taken captive. The boy wonders what manner of creature he has found, so we take the apple and the busy connoisseur to the pool and find a variety of its more familiar relatives. A slug is, more or less, a snail without its suit on, and there are more puzzles in the clan than my small son cares, now, to know about.

Consider the moistness of the slug, for instance, and the trail of slime it leaves. In snails, this secretion is what forms the shell, hardening on exposure to the air, growing on an axis in whorl or wheel. Both snail and slug are road builders: The glistening path they make is a film of mucus put down by a gland at the forepart of the foot. And the foot itself is a marvel of locomotion, capable of oozing almost in haste over rock and debris, delicate enough to walk on the underside of the surface film of water.

There are both gill-breathing snails and those with lung sacs. Among the former, the foot, or a portion of it called the operculum, can be withdrawn in times of stress to block entry to the shell, leaving the door barred effectively and the occupant snug inside.

In another time, this operculum was called an eye stone and was used by healers to treat patients with foreign bodies in their eyes. The eye stone was placed under the sufferer's lid, and somehow— probably by counter irritation that stimulated the flow of tears— magically accomplished the removal of the offending material. The real wonder is not that such a thing should be effective but that it ever should become known. What manner of physician first thought to put a fragment of snail foot into an injured eye as treatment? And why?

Among the snails, there were created males, and females, and those that were both: true hermaphrodites, with complete, complex, reproductive systems of both sexes. In the laboratory, such a hermaphroditic snail may be established as self-fertile, yet in nature it seems rarely so. The biologically independent slug still seeks its kind and mates the one way and the other. Again, why?

And why, for that matter, does my smallest child pore with fascinated frown over these strange matters of the gastropods while his stalwart brother, grown curious at our study, drops the apple as though it burned him when he touches the clammy subject of it all?

79

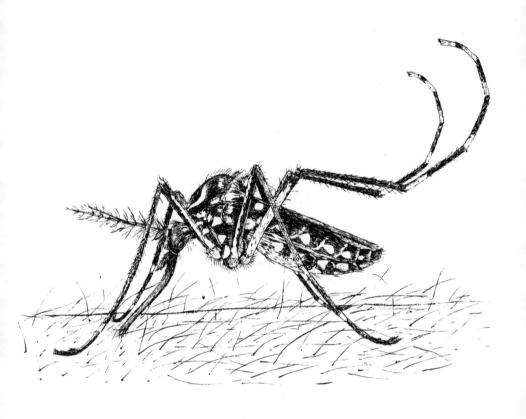

*T*he air is like summer, but the golden Grecian light on the terrace is old October. White bones of birches begin to show through the thinning yellow flamework of their leaves, and already the butternuts are stark and bare. Still, the coffee trees and silver maples are as green as August, and presently there is another reminder that cold, sere, buttoned autumn is not yet fully here: A final generation of mosquitoes rises from the pool and seeks the banquet of warm blood that is essential to starting another cycle.

It seems a process too dubious to tell, but there it is—without the hot meal, the eggs do not develop properly. And at this time of year, there had better be small delay; at least that seems to be the philosophy of the current buzzing plague. A singing mosquito is dangerous to unprotected skin. Only the female plays that chitinous fiddle on her back, and, of course, only the female bites.

Still, unseemly haste seems out of place at this time of year. Cold weather does not mean the end of the mosquito clan. Mosquitoes swarm north of the Arctic Circle; some varieties will lay their eggs on the snow; and some larvae endure the winter frozen fast in ice. And when sun and moisture are in appropriate conjunction, the whole cycle from egg to egg again may be gone through in as little as two weeks.

But these latecomers are flourishing by accident in my pool. All summer long, the tiny eggs are laid, the wrigglers hatch, and the fish gorge happily and grow fat. I don't know how many wrigglers such a fish can eat in a summer, but surely it is up in the numbers ordinarily associated with astrophysics or public taxation. All summer, female mosquitoes, complying with ancestral urges, labor mightily at reproduction, resulting in startling growth records for my little fish. But recently the fish were taken up and carried to the indoor tank, and the pool left to its own devices.

The products of its own devices are apparent—a pell-mell generation of mosquitoes, eager, insistent, and hungry, with time pressing hard on their heels. Here, in microcosm, is a demonstration in ordered environment gone suddenly wild when the control mechanism —the fish—is taken away. Here, if you are brave enough to be frightened by little things, is a small story of disaster. All it takes is to multiply mosquitoes to the size of eagles or the ferocity of shrews to make the horror genuine.

81

*F*oraging for the fireplace, the woodsman moves a log that has lain too long among the leaves and unroofs a cauldron that is instantly aboil with rage. The Siamese cat recoils momentarily, ears flattened, before coming back grittily at the shrew. But the cat's brief hesitation was enough, and the mite of rage is gone among the leaves or down a musty tunnel where a root decayed, a tiny arrow moving almost faster than the eye can see in the gray day.

Except for the cat's reaction, the flurry might easily have been ignored. But now there is a pause while woodsman and cat speculate. Cats have been forever the enemy of shrews, although the tiny beasts are rarely eaten. Once, it was thought that shrews were poisonous; and if only their disposition were counted, this was true. Consider that the cat, at twelve pounds, might be a coyote's match; but if the shrew were the cat's size, no mammal on our continent could feel safe.

The glimpse in the leaves was too brief to tell, but it matters little whether the beast at bay was *Sorex* or *Microsorex*. He was less than four inches long, and nearly half of that was tail. If he were the smaller shrew, the pigmy, then he was the rarer of the two and the smallest mammal we have here.

No matter which, he was of an order callect insect eaters. And he will even eat what tries to eat him back. There is a record of three shrews imprisoned together under one jar. Two of them promptly set upon the third and ate it. By nightfall, one of those left had eaten the other. And again, in captivity, one pigmy shrew ate twenty larger shrews, a white-footed mouse, a red-backed mouse, and another pigmy shrew, all in just ten days.

Alienation is not such a new thing. It can be a way of life in lower animals and is possibly more frightening because of it. Here is a consuming rage, hate if you prefer, so great that it even overshadows lust. And yet, of all the little brothers of the wild, the shrew is the only one I have known that may die suddenly of nothing more than fright. The one reaction is as characteristic of the shrew as the other.

83

Suddenly it seems that a pestilence has wiped out great banks of trees among the conifer islands that stand so darkly green along the prairie marshes. Among the blue-black of the spruces are naked branches stark against the chilly sky. But it is not a plague, only the annual divestiture of the tamaracks, which drop their needle leaves in autumn, even as the maples.

Most so-called evergreens go through this process in stages. So many needles drop this year, so many next, and so on. The fallen are replaced, and the trees are never visibly reduced, although the carpeting of dry needles beneath them gradually deepens. But in October, the tamaracks begin to change color. Their green pales and signals clearly what was hard to tell from a distance before—which marshly islet is spruce and which tamarack.

This American larch has other contrasts and comparisons. Spruces rise in peat grown heavy and solid, but tamaracks may be found growing on a mossy bog that is scarcely more than a surface mat of vegetation advancing over open water. A tamarack's roots may be only a foot deep, but they extend around it for a distance greater than the height of the tree. And from the wandering rootlets may spring new trees, fifty feet or more from the parent, in a manner foreign to most conifers.

A determination to endure is behind this. Tamaracks cannot bear the dark; their seeds will not grow in the trees' own shade. On top of that, the seeds will sprout only in constant moistness, but will generally die in standing water. Again, the tamarack's thin bark will not stand against fire; even a burning off of grasses will kill it where it stands. But where it stands, of course, is on the quaking bog, inches away from water, and so the fire seldom comes.

A man might consider these things and wonder. Did the defense against the weakness develop, in time, to show a way to survival? Or did the weakness develop because of the perpetual and undemanding defense? And is this true only of tamaracks?

85

*T*hanksgiving has been cited as a holiday so wholly concerned with subjective American emotional experience that no one foreign to the culture can ever expect to understand it. The observation does not require any great discernment; the same might be said of Guy Fawkes Day in one quarter and May Day in another. The stature of the tradition is better measured by saying that understanding it only adds to the confusion.

Take the turkey, for instance, with which the American holiday has been inseparably identified ever since that first of September, Old Style, in the year after Captain Christopher Jones closed his eyes and payed his miserable barkentine through Pollack's Rip into Provincetown Harbor. Because not quite all those first crops were a failure, there was reason for rejoicing together.

"There being an abundance of wild turkies which do amaze us with their speed of foot in the woods," the Winslow family archives notes, "our governor sent four men in fowling. They four in one day killed as much fowl as, with a little help, served the company almost a week." The little help, it should be added, included five deer, but no matter. The turkey's the thing, and, in 1621, it became the feature of the first Thanksgiving because it was available and because the marksmen of Plimouth Plantation could hit it on the ground.

In this day, there surely are traditionalists who feel the holiday can best be noted only with eastern wild turkey, *Meleagris gallopavo,* but of these people, only the few who are very rich or very lucky— or most likely both—are able to maintain the mighty myth. For while the myth was being fostered, the eastern wild turkey almost disappeared. Recently it has been coaxed back as a wild species in a number of states, largely because a handful of faithful in Pennsylvania managed over the years to keep poultry experts from "improving" the initial strain. But even now, there are probably something fewer than half a million eastern turkeys alive; while each year, one hundred million of their fat, dowdy, mostly-white-meat descendants go to market.

Yet, in a way, the legend has come full circle. The wild turkey of 1621 was the main dish because it was there; the wild turkey now is the trophy bird, the rare and long-sought climax of many a year's shooting. And what is here is the rectangular fellow with the drumsticks as thick as your arm, done neatly up in the butcher's case—now, as then, the cheapest readily available source of animal protein for the day of the year that is famed throughout the world for exceptional cuisine.

$\mathcal{A}$t morning now the aging veterans of the insect world are torpid and only move, joints creaking, when the sun has warmed within them recollections of hot summer days. A bumblebee buzzes with vague irritation and wanders away when rooted out of the grass by a rake. The liveried hornets sprawl on the elm bark like yeomen in their cups, their weaponry askew, and may be swatted with impunity.

But at noon it is summer again, and over the pool there is the splendor of iridescent dragonfly wings moving coolly with the incredible flash and dive of aerobatics that drive even martins to despair.

Devil's darning needles, they were called in my boyhood. They would sew your mouth shut, it was said, if you told one lie too many; they would do the same to your eyelids if you were apprehended peeking in the door of the girls' locker room.

It may serve you, if you are pleased with innocent intellectual accomplishments, to know that the order Odonata, which is made up of the dragonflies and damselflies, can be made orderly if you remember that the former come to rest with their four handsomely veined wings outspread; the latter hold their wings up together over their backs. Both have legs that are unused to walking but that form a hairy basket for scooping up lesser insects in flight.

All the dragonfly life cycle is associated with water, and in the dozen or so pupal stages, the nymphs are important citizens in the feeding-and-fed-upon community, occupying an area midway between mosquito larvae and hungry ducks. But in November the green and gold of dragonflies serve a higher purpose, especially for humans who sense in the shortening days the threat of winter that looms ahead for all whose blood is warm.

You see the Aeshnid female, fresh from her nuptial flight, drilling into the lily stem at the waterline to place the eggs that hold promise of next summer's flights, and suddenly you are reassured. Nothing truly ends. All this will come again.

89

About the Illustrations

12   Gopher, *Citellus tridecemlineatus*. This animal has scores of common names, among them flag squirrel (for its 13 stripes and starlike spots). Its hibernation is one of the most complete among mammals; sometimes the animal never awakens. John Muir reported finding a gopher "frozen solid in its snug grassy nest, in the middle of a store of nearly a peck of wheat it had carefully gathered . . . . Its life had passed away without the slightest struggle."

14   Red-breasted nuthatch, *Sitta canadensis*. Smaller and less common than the white-breasted nuthatch, this bird is primarily an insect eater, though it occasionally feeds at feeding stations. The species is quite tame and willingly feeds near humans.

16   Norway spruce, *Picea abies*. This is the tree most Civil War-era farmers planted for decoration and windbreaks, replacing the native species they had felled.

18   Meadow mouse, *Microtus pennsylvanicus*. The female begins breeding at one month and annually produces up to 13 litters of four to eight young. Each mouse eats its own weight in plant material daily, and populations of 12,000 mice per acre have been recorded.

20   Red fox, *Vulpes fulva*. This fox mates in January and February, perhaps for life, and may well be the world's greatest destroyer of mice.

22   The constellation Taurus, the Bull. The Pleiades star cluster, on the Bull's shoulder, consists of more than 500 stars, the brightest of which are each more than 800 times larger than the sun.

24   White-tailed deer, *Odocoileus virginianus*. Antlers are usually shed by the end of January; new antler growth begins in April or May. An average deer consumes six to eight pounds of browse daily. Some 100 trees and shrubs are browsed, including yew, white cedar, and hemlock.

26   Prairie spotted skunk, *Spilogale putorius*. Smaller and slimmer than the striped skunk, and common in most of the United States, its fur is marketed as civet cat. This skunk is shown in its characteristic "handstand" habit, in which the animal—in play or bluff—throws its hindquarters into the air and stands or walks on its front feet.

30   Sugar maple, *Acer saccharum*. Maple sap contains two and a half percent sugar, and an average tree yields 20 gallons, enough to make a half gallon of syrup or four pounds of sugar.

32   Ring-necked pheasant, *Phasianus colchicus*. The eyes of this game bird,

an introduced native of China and Korea, often but not always close at death.

34 Mourning cloak, *Nymphalis antiopa*. Both sexes have deep maroon wings with yellow borders and blue spots on the upper surfaces. Adults often emerge before the snow is melted.

36 Woodfern, *Dryopteris spinulosa*. These beautiful and unusually hardy ferns survive transplanting well. The fronds are sometimes cut and sold for ornament.

38 Spadefoot toad, *Scaphiopus* sp. This stout, nocturnal, relatively smooth toad is found in most of the United States. The toad the author encountered, however, was probably an American toad, *Bufo americanus*. *Bufo*'s skin and slime are distasteful to many enemies; *Scaphiopus*'s are not.

40 Earthworm, *Lumbricus terrestris*. Darwin contended that an acre of soil may contain 63,000 earthworms, which, in a year, can bring 18 tons of soil to the surface. A robin has ended this earthworm's career as a landscape architect.

42 Bindweed, *Convolvulus arvensis*. The author claims his typewriter is not quite as venerable as the antique Sholes & Glidden model the artist has depicted.

44 Snowshoe hare, *Lepus americanus*. Called the varying hare because it turns from red-brown in summer to pure white—except for black ear tips—in winter, *Lepus* is known for topping young conifers.

46 Raccoon, *Procyon lotor*. The average weight is 30 pounds, though specimens of more than 60 pounds have been recorded. If caught young, coons are easily tamed and make excellent pets.

50 Dandelion, *Taraxacum officinale*. This native of Eurasia has made itself at home thoughout North and South America.

52 Brown-headed cowbird, *Molothrus ater*. The name comes from the bird's habit of collecting insects from the backs of cattle.

54 Anglewing, genera *Polygonia*, *Nymphalis*, and *Anaea*. From the chrysalis, it's difficult to tell which anglewing this creature is about to become.

56 Woodchuck, *Marmota monax*. Fabled harbinger of spring. Like other members of the squirrel family, the woodchuck frequently climbs trees, often to escape pursuers but sometimes just to sun itself.

58 Blue jay, *Cyanocitta cristata*; and monarch, *Danaus plexippus*. It's unlikely anything but a totally inexperienced jay would completely swallow a butterfly before discovering it to be unpalatable.

60 Mud puppy, *Necturus* sp. When its fluffy red gills are not extended, the mud puppy more closely resembles its relatives the salamanders and newts. Reported to be good eating, the mud puppy lives about twenty years.

62 Bumblebee, *Bombus* sp. There are numerous species of *Bombus,* most of which are gold and black.

66 Bear grass, *Yucca glauca.* This yucca is native to the Southwest but is often planted as an ornamental. An alcoholic beverage is made from the fermented juice of some yuccas.

68 Indigo bunting, *Passerina cyanea.* The plain brown female and brilliant blue male are frequently seen on telephone wires along country roads.

72 The artist used her imagination to come up with this Druid, but the object of his reverence is clearly a sycamore.

74 White-footed mouse, *Peromyscus leucopus.* Like this inebriated specimen, *Peromyscus* often takes shelter in houses during winter but vacates the premises in summer.

76 New England aster, *Aster novae-angliae.* Even a sober textbook writer was moved to comment: "Too beautiful to be destroyed if area it occupies is not needed by other plants."

78 Slug, *Deroceras reticulatum.* Introduced from Europe in the last century, this slug has spread over the entire eastern United States and made the acquaintance of Greg Mastrangelo, the artist's second cousin.

80 Mosquito, *Aedes* sp. The bite is only the beginning. *Culex* often carries filariasis, *Anopheles* carries malaria, and *Aedes* carries yellow fever.

82 Long-tailed shrew, *Sorex cinereus.* According to Hartley H. T. Jackson, this shrew "is an active, vicious, voracious, high-strung, and restless little imp . . . . A mated pair may live together without much fighting, but put two or three others together and they fight savagely." The vast majority of the shrew's diet, however, consists of insects.

84 Tamarack, *Larix laricina.* The tamarack grows to 80 feet in swamps and bogs. Pyramidal when young, it becomes open-topped with age.

86 Wild turkey, *Meleagris gallopavo.* This game bird is usually placed in the subspecies *silvestris* to separate it from the domestic bird, with which it interbreeds freely. Though wary now, wild turkeys were poultry-yard pests in Colonial New England.

88 Dragonfly, *Libellula* sp. Between 5,000 and 10,000 different kinds of dragonfly are known today; this one has sealed the lips of Bradley Forkash, another of the artist's cousins.

A Sand County Almanac Illustrated

Aldo Leopold, author
Tom Algire, photographer

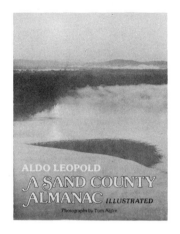

Now, in *A Sand County Almanac Illustrated,* Aldo Leopold's timeless words are given a new dimension with the addition of Tom Algire's superb illustrations. We can see in Algire's sensitive photographs how completely he shares and understands Leopold's love of the land and belief that man must learn to live in harmony with it. Through the seasons, Tom Algire has photographed the area made famous by *A Sand County Almanac.* The result is sixty-four elegant photographs that reaffirm the Leopold spirit as they capture the quiet majesty of a beautiful and peaceful place.

160 pages, 9″ x 12″, hardbound, 64 color photographs.